MW00467424

Blinking Ephemeral Valentine

.99
7/

2020 - 1462

Blinking Ephemeral Valentine

Joni Wallace

Four Way Books
Tribeca

Copyright © 2011 by Joni Wallace
No part of this book may be used or reproduced in any manner
without written permission except in the case of brief quotations
embodied in critical articles and reviews.

Please direct all inquiries to:
Editorial Office
Four Way Books
POB 535, Village Station
New York, NY 10014
www.fourwaybooks.com

Library of Congress Cataloging-in-Publication Data

Wallace, Joni.
  Blinking ephemeral valentine / Joni Wallace.
    p. cm.
  ISBN 978-1-935536-09-3 (pbk. : alk. paper)
  I. Title.
  PS3623.A4433B55 2011
  811'.6--dc22

                    2010032294

This book is manufactured in the United States of America
and printed on acid-free paper.

Four Way Books is a not-for-profit literary press. We are grateful for the assistance
we receive from individual donors, public arts agencies, and private foundations.

Funding for this book was provided in part by a generous donation
in memory of John J. Wilson.

This publication is made possible with public funds
from the National Endowment for the Arts

NATIONAL
ENDOWMENT
FOR THE ARTS
A great nation
deserves great art

Distributed by University Press of New England
One Court Street, Lebanon, NH 03766

[clmp]   We are a proud member of the Council of Literary Magazines and Presses.

TABLE OF CONTENTS

One

Two

Three

Four

Notes

One

You are here,

map says,

big toy world

ASSEMBLAGE WITH FIREFLIES

Love the world, the plumb moon
that longs to break or give out.
A door slams but the house is quiet,
blizzard of nothing.
When you are sure there are no visitors,
you bang the machines, *bang bang*.
But you are not dying, that darling sleeps
elsewhere and precious little.
You should lay it on your eyes, that and the windows.
And trees multiply, a sylvan greening.
And clouds score the distance that holds them.
And fireflies, a slipstream, spinners and jacks.

STAR-SPANGLED VALENTINE SHAGGED IN DRAB

Crescent train, a.m., heads west,
little *o* for a headlight, little robber's
gashed glare. I put my ear
to the singing, lean in to going.
America, I've learned
your image traffic—ashen pigeons
trilling electric lines, razor wire looped
over fences, satellites blinking
into gasoline rings.
I fell hard for the Wide Open,
your scrap yards and tree-lined rivers,
parking lots etched into prairies.
All this inside myself, a broken
bottle gleaming. Tell me a story,
begin with a flag unfurled
and a sun-warmed body of cows,
black/white and black.
Tell me another where you're something
flamed and spinning, top or superhero,
now the ticker tape fall,
now the remnant float,
a boxcar graffitied, aluminum clouds.

RED AND BLUE PLANETS

What we're drawn to is proof enough:
these pills, other acts of disappearance.
I've written a song about a girl who swallowed the blue planets:
Kevlar, Caroline, O Beautiful Bomb.
So perfectly haplessly cruel the world we've made.
Let's meet back here in 5 minutes, you say, you always say.
I'll bring the Lite-Brite.
I'll bring the hole in my heart, a white star burning.
More and more, the rock show.
Venus rising is a glass wrecking ball,
inside red harbors, red sails.

HOLIDAY

Despite the weather I tell you everything
I'll never say to you, and I keep swaying,
red plastic cup in hand, until I'm not myself entirely.
You look nice under the mirror ball, *sparkle sparkle*
swirl, and how like the squall, your face
a cast of shade reeling.
Please open the sky with a nail or a hammer or a nail.
I want to see the moon's umbrella glory the lawn.
It rains, it rains in the suburbs,
on sidewalks and fences
where glitterati crows imagine themselves into trees.

EASTER IN SNOW ANGELS

Outside the gate so many cars,
whole cities, slate panes of glass.
We take residence.
Hang and misnail.
We watch as twilight drags the strip,
lane after lane stained
with television glow.
Sometimes I think I understand
love like an image I don't cast
but when I run toward it my shadow
contorts: crippled king, queen of knees.
This is an awful month, the sleet
and snowmelt and snow angels
glinting from fields.
Draw x's where their eyes should be,
you say, you can't squint another minute.
Camera *click*, a wingscrape.
I am twirling my coat.

Pornographic valentine

When were you gone? Once upon I caught you, a bruise, a bled
tattoo, *love, love*, Love, the weather clear, we were drinking. Now
love's an engine that drags the dark, a smut-stained arpeggio,
scarslit moon in its curtain of ether. Past stations, past platforms,
mercy mirrors me a kiss, tongueless, part extinction, part drink.

Valentine with saints and sharps

There's not much to do
but sit on the asphalt-of-little-sorrows
in white plastic chairs.
If we connect goldfoil
dot-to-dot: Roman
candles ablaze.
Sweet Sebastian,
his back knit with arrows,
mother-of-pearl Cecilia
in her rented wedding dress,
a skull cap, and oh
the trick floor evermore.
Miserable comforts, hairpins,
saint-shaped scars graven
into arms outstretched,
glass eyes, a trayful,
the holy-shit-fires,
bells bells
and a choir, tripwired.
Now the lesser saints,
wrong skyjackers
dropped from the cumuli,
sharps in the statuary.

Snow globe with Frank O'Hara and arboretum

Say what you want, Frank,
forever asking after shimmering names
of things, it's cheery enough in here. If we're left
to boredom in sad-wheeling not-air, why not, you're
a skater and I'm fourteen, your mittened hand's forever
next to mine on the ice rail. Geraniums like red lanterns
that row toward Christmas, everything lit and backlit,
so real, better than blinkers outside splintering the
cake glass. Sphere of loneliness, idiomatic vacuum
filled with the sound of nothing/snow,
is there a carol for ever-leaving,
one for the ice starlings studding the arboretum?
Cold enough to breathe now, we keep small,
everglitter felled on likeness of trees.

DUCT-TAPE VALENTINE

Remember our best night? Not drowning, not the self-same gasping
as a makeshift blast broadcast through gaping windows, river and
skyline turned over, pigeons piercing the surface like reverse rain.
Outside the evening zephyrs, similar scenes. If I imagine you moving
to open a car door, I get in. *There are whole days left to destroy*, you say.
Now we are far away, we are breaking, dull thuds on a stage.
Hello, hello, hello, hello.

Swim

At four you could make yourself
invisible and stay that way, make a world
out of egg cartons and sequins, here a picnic,
here a glass town. Sometimes you still see
inside your head, a filmstrip of sticker states
and striped shirts, you are parachute-girl,
you are dance-girl, you are swagger,
you are swim.
Then nothing. Disappeared.
Float for hours, happy as it is.
You can't tell if the air is moving.
Clouds stretch into a chain.
No ghost, no broken boat, no swan looks away.

Reel-to-reel

Pox on the living.
Movie prize of some long
ago actress, not me,
and she shall witness
our breaths fly out
in a minor scene,
waxshine of stiletto heels,
fur voltage, radiant
ringlets ringed in smoke,
do you have a light?
Enter Mr. Satie
and his cupful of sloe,
enter a room where I lose
you to the *plink*
of a piano player,
a bar sign scintillating
boite de jazz /
tilt view almost missed
as dusk steels the set
set into blankness,
my exquisite wound.
This the part where the credits roll:
hand of glances,

catch-as-catch-can.

Please place your headphones in the seatback in front of you.

Please exit through the doors marked EXIT.

Step out onto the boulevard.

It could be this or any city.

Narrative poem left out in the rain

Choose an ending
from the Book of Endings,
which the most guttural,
which the most vanished-into-air?
Dog circles,
red-blue-yellow-violet
halos above a Rainbird,
a mischief of mice,
too-fast mouse,
a-bit-of-sock-mouse,
a ladder to nowhere,
bad-fucking-luck
in a tin can of rain.
Mother, mother,
beginning of sadness,
you are, an apron to sing it,
a house and a housecoat,
part light, part rust
dismantling the frame.
Walk into the backdrop.
Screen porch, willow tree's
silhouette below a marbled
thunderhead. Alone,
I make a door

in the jewelweed.
So summer ends:
junebug.

Narrative poem left out in the rain, exploded view

World of pieces, gazes, astonished mice.
Sidereal streaks in the side yard,
ruthless sun conjuring concentric circles.
Droplets and drops, tremble of that,
gossamer leaves sewn into your skirt.

Everywhere like Paris

Talk me down if you can.
I'll come back in a canary-yellow taxi,
my arms filled with flowers, my butterfly bandages
right as the cold and iridescent drizzle
on the breeze and bums and benches
where I am not waving, not holding my clear
plastic bag like a brilliant future kiss.
Who says a skyscape
is the geometry of angels,
who says a pinwheel
of particulates turning?
It's getting so I can't tell
a pageant from a parade, day
upon day of warplane aerobatics
over roof terraces, little girls
poised on the lips of pools, pink
Emerson radios crooning,
balcony after balcony
of holographic gun-spray
imitating shrapnel, hey sister,
tell me anything against after.
I line it all with a chalk that's neon,
make an architecture for *ledge*.
When the pigeons come,

gray fists and bits of violet,
I let them know.
Gravity gathers, endless as mud.

Valentine behind door number one

>
> *To whom it may concern—*
> Do not open.
> *One good cut,* envelope says,
> to prove it, *and we'll bleed stars,*
> *you and I.*
> > *handkerchief / tourniquet*

Two

into air,

       invisible kingdom

Still life with Jack

Come into the sable night,
thing-witch with your strap
of knives, a blue-black bat
shadowboxing your hand.
What you want starts out
wicked, lit mouth, triangle eye,
but then the light won't disappear,
you wander through a window,
you begin carving
constellations, houses below.
Smaller hours, you are tired,
what room, what beds?
Moths come, ghosts
in their ghost light.
You are six or you are seven
and counting, you have made
little airplanes of aspirins and glue.
It's a trick to solo in your charcoal dress.

Detail from Still life with Jack (1)

Glister goes the darkness,
a theater you step into.
White is visible, you are, too,
in a pillbox hat, patent shoes
and hands come apart.
Fly low, flathat, a sudden
weather shapes the distance.
Not one single metaphor.

Detail from Still life with Jack (2)

Filament of thought.
Stop.
Heron flashlit
in the cellophane air.
Stop.
Beveled bridge,
breakneck wind.
Stop.
Paper shreds from a room above this one.

DROWN

Endless moths.
Soft whir of bodies.
I'll trace for you flight patterns,
vapor trails circumvolve.
Like galaxies, unreal.
Slip-of-a-girl in a smocked dress,
cut your circlet from the dotted lines,
may the chitin dust bejewel you.
Comes the back-of-the-throat ghost.
Comes the rain.
Lake etched by boats.
Days fishtail, lost lures,
flinty dreams of flight
in the water box under.
I said corset of fishbone,
I said heart-sponge.
Or, here is the mind,
palace of tears.
Leaves on the cottonwoods
turn over, silver bodies.
Nothing rises.
My own sunken hand blooms beautiful.
Imagine Lazarus' resurrection
in the throat,
and just after,
his terrible hands.

Valentine behind door number two

Here lies the starlit heart
housed in scarlet shingles.
Blood-bright, the socket.
White piano of ribs.
For you a lightbox to hold them.
Pry it open and the panorama leaks out,
twinkles too.

Three

shovel the rubble

VALENTINE WITH BROKEN BIRDS

Enclosed find pieces of the starling flown flat
against my window, that flimflam unseeable too
vivid to enter. They don't go back there,
the killdeer, not the swallows and not the rooks,
not the sparrows or the run-and-pause plover,
neither the red birds nor the red cinderellas.
Enter here the courtyard of hollow-boned wings.
Place your clavicle, a mandible, behind the parchment:
a shadow pterodactyl posts there.

ACCIDENTAL FOR J

Dusk slat-shot through shutters.
I count words between louvers, my *hush-hush*
eye exam, bedclothes my template.
Room empty, so also the innocent air.
I can't remember if the clock chimes anytime ever.
If it snows I'm dressed like Christmas, I'm lit,
I'm drinking Red Rockets and oh how they glare.
Here is where I think of you.
Here is a picture, negative, x-ray, reverse.

SELF-PORTRAIT WITH WEATHER

Well-tuned, churring, yellow jackets blow among
trees.

Buy me a dress for my take-away hat, a plot to go with them,
a carton of clods.

Be beauty, blinks the mirror-mirror, a treble winging over me.

Drape a cape, the world is gone.

On the window, on the flashing, a branchlet.

ECLIPSE ECLIPSE

1.

Phosphor, give me more—

fine-boned edge glow,

tinsel crown halo scored.

2.

Lest you think this the end of landscape,

look at Earth's intaglio illumined overhead.

3.

I love the shadow puppets,

those who enter the Cowpalace

and those who do not.

4.

Image holds

a flame / flicker.

5.

You drive, you are miles more dangerous.

6.

x marks the sound out.

Valentine with girl falling and music

Once upon a time a skeleton girl who fell to earth singing.
Below her a lake, dazzling fish, elongated fins. Then
glass slippers, a scorpion luminescing link-to-link.
*I'll raise an ocean, a phosphorescent tide, an ice-colored kite sunk
into ice-colored heavens,* says she. Gravity, our forecast, our
lovely-engine-slightly-gunned, miss you, kiss you.

Zoetrope, small horses and animals

Indelible horses.
From your lips a whorl,
a vellum soliloquy of stops
and sirens bowl down.
Princess Hold Out,
around your neck
a string of caterpillars
and small figurines, you make
the tower from which you
plunge the practice birds,
vermillion-stained, aviators all,
shoe-shined confetti to litter
earth the earth the earth
a silver-wheel whirring.
Finally a bridle, your ruined boots
and thunderous lashes.
Dangle low. Gallop.

Valentine behind door number three with cumulonimbus

Beside the world a tower,
a deer threads through.
How high the spectacle,
melody inside, pearl
molecules warbling.
Unmake it, stick and hollow.
Saltlick, alabaster hare, porcelain winds.
These to sing, so very.
Repeat.

VALENTINE FOR A CAT AND FIDDLE

How I have wanted you, your high wires and high balloons.
I do not always. Love enters the room disguised as a spoon.
My plate, my plate, my plate never is. Jet scrim, gray
cement moon, insomniac cow. Kill the lights, please. Cut.

Four

string lights,

snowlight

National monument

1.

Wish yourself inside
the ornamental deer,
veneer of and spots
floating in the reservoir,
water breaking the edges.
In the time lapse of drift forever
a lasso across your shoulder
and in your pocket
a fly's wing
on which to sketch
your S.O.S.,
a ribbed dog.

2.

Things you will need:
nightglasses;
cerulean stain;
best gloves;
any number of ladders.

3.

Stand up in the black hollow:
moldable sounds of

a perfect ocean
under which you believe
an incandescent carousel
circles.

4.

When you have finished
hold your reflection up
to the keyhole:
kits and toy soldiers
in the ragweed, a crossing.
Says so, the bullet-sprayed
sign, shape of antlers
or black branches,
wind making it disappear.

5.

Here the poem whistles
an elk to the shoreline.
Whistle, whistle and another,
another, a queue of, hold onto.

MONTANA

Forgive clouds passing. To this place
you've come with your bag of boots,
an invisible pasture in your pocket
and before you the greenest grass you've never known.
Geese cast off before you, more gather
at the sides of the barn.
It's your first part in a Western,
you're brilliant in a neck scarf, a petticoat,
you sing like a shiny postcard of yourself
I love the clouds   clouds that pass by   over there
  over there   those lovely clouds
a clutter of goats to your left, small bells
and a bleat to your right.

VALENTINE FOR A SAD-EYED UNKNOWABLE LOTTO CLERK

Dear. I flung away my goodbyes, flywheels and marigolds all, of those midair still hanging souvenirs and petals I'll press into pies. Goldfish, swift fist, catapult disguised as a flame, I found your casement, bas relief, in the grass. Gentle weathervane, you lie where you languished, fang-throated, glamorously finned, row upon row from your wet city at night. Morning guillotines, oars between us. Can you hear me, sweetheart? Love. Yours. Always.

LET'S BUILD A CORRAL

Meanwhile, meanwhile,
braids everywhere, ebullient cattle.
I'm six steps into the thicket.
You're branding with big and little *B*'s.
Of course we're wild, rouged
down to our ankles, stripped up
to our horses, grass full of snakes,
grass full of moles, mole holes.
Nail and raze, come now, blaze.

Uncut year

Wade right out in the Year of Excellent Clouds.
Another evening, another park, another horse
on which to ride. See the sky reflected
on the tear films of an owlet? Paint a thing,
trompe-l'oeil, it comes. Trace the sun,
do not look, see it see it without your eyes.

CAMERA OBSCURA

I'll tumble the drinks while you
take a Sharpie and mark hillside sheep,
round as soap bubbles, on the wall.
We are smiling, we are emptying the world,
we try to look clean. Straight out's
chroma, almost permanent, wide open.
No hand, no box can hold it.

PURPLE PLASTIC DECODER VALENTINE

All these hours behind
a window, a glass or a pistol
in my hand, laconic levelings
in an aisle striped like a landing.

But in air every motion's slowed,
that beautiful pilot at point-blank range
a beautiful pilot forever.
And see how the wing lights stutter,
          skipjack message for the azure.

Shhh, that's a secret
(spin again).

It will fall on us, this sky, a riot-sad serenade.
After that a jewel color not the sun.

This is also a secret.

So let our lies sound out!
Love like a plane-shaped
hole punched into asphalt,
a sudden engine deadman down,

our enameled swansong
dropped into one indeterminate sentence,
jubilant dun, chalk mark
midair.

TWENTY-FIRST CENTURY BEST BOY

I'm the hero and I'm the stiff-legged lamb,
swallowtails kiting over me like paper flames.
Radiant boy! Bring me a green-bottle cloud chamber,
particles to string the future and the future's vapor wake.
This is a story for living, a good one,
insects draped across doorways while her engine *ticks ticks*
and I play the century in as chiaroscuro,
bare-bulb sun on my left.
Body electric, he mouths, then *abacus beads, quicksilver on wire.*
Odd how he moves, traceless, now erased.
I in the hallway, I in the graphite street.

Poem for this speed

Miles from here we are palimpsest ghosts
on a throne of chrome, a vacancy half lit in the ruby wattage
      of tail lights
while a neon snow seeps over the long blank of blacktop.
It's a day like any other, planets locked in grid.
Before long one absence we remember, not holy,
appears (web of vein-work, tiny flutter, ribs inside a veil).
I do not know you, but still.
We trade our skins for glassine sleeves.
The east and west join us, we take in our arms.
It's a zero weather, like winter, chill ions spark
through broken windshields.
The drive says surgery.
Mottled deer, somnambulant sheep,
boughs cut through. Pass as scars.

Notes and Dedications

In the poem MONTANA, italicized lines belong to Charles Baudelaire. The phrases "big toy world," "the weather clear, we were drinking" and "hand of glances" (ONE, PORNOGRAPHIC VALENTINE and REEL-TO-REEL) are adapted lines from Paul Celan, *Glottal Stop*. The phrase "shovel the rubble" (THREE) belongs to Heather McHugh.

SNOW GLOBE WITH FRANK O'HARA AND ARBORETUM contains two misprisions derived from Frank O'Hara, *The Collected Poems of Frank O'Hara*.

RED AND BLUE PLANETS is dedicated to Carl Petersen.

REEL-TO-REEL is dedicated to Kimberly Brusuelas.

STILL LIFE WITH JACK is dedicated to Ann McGlinn.

DROWN is dedicated to Richard Greenfield.

VALENTINE WITH BROKEN BIRDS owes a shadow to Matthea Harvey.

ZOETROPE, SMALL HORSES AND ANIMALS is dedicated to Lucia Iurino.

UNCUT YEAR is dedicated to Renz Iurino.

I'd like to thank the following people: Mark Levine,
Richard Shelton, Patricia Goedicke, Stephen Dunn and
Dean Young. Also Lisa Bowden, Martha Rhodes, Sally Ball,
Ryan Murphy and everyone at Four Way Books, Joan Houlihan,
Frances Sjoberg and Ann McGlinn for their help and input.

Special thanks to Scott Rhea for the use of his image
"When Horses Dream."

My gratitude to Mary Jo Bang for her selection of this manuscript.

To Mom and Dad, who insisted on poetry and music: thank you.

To Kathryn, Charlotte, Lucia and Renz: all my love.

And to John: one tree.

ACKNOWLEDGMENTS

The author thanks the editors of the following journals in which these poems first appeared, some in earlier versions:

Barrow Street; *Boston Review*; *Conduit*; *Connotation Press, An Online Artifact*; *Crazyhorse*; *Forklift, Ohio*; *Laurel Review*; and *No Tell Motel*.

Special thanks to the Arizona Commission on the Arts and the Vermont Studio Center for a fellowship and a residency, respectively, which allowed for the completion of many of these poems.

Joni Wallace grew up in Los Alamos, New Mexico, and Moab, Utah. She is the author of *Redshift* (Kore Press, 2000) and her recent poems appear in *Barrow Street*; *Boston Review*; *Conduit*; *Connotations Press, An Online Artifact*; *Forklift, Ohio*; *Laurel Review* and *No Tell Motel*. She holds an MFA from the University of Montana and currently lives in the Southwest with her husband, John, and their two young children.